5 Steps to Better Blurbs:
Crafting Dynamic Descriptions that Sell

By Julie C. Gilbert

May this book help you on your writer journey.

~Julie C. Gilbert

devyaschildren@gmail.com

Dedication:

To the lovely people who let me play with their blurbs.

And to independent authors everywhere.
Keep following your dreams.

Special thanks: Alex Reacher for the cover design idea.

Table of Contents:

Introduction:

Dear Authors, Friends, and Friendly Strangers,

I've been called the Blurb Queen, but I'm more like the Court Jester, wielding words with wit, wisdom, and weirdness where appropriate. In any case, I'm also a teacher, so I'm going to define blurbs and show you my process. Next, I'll lay out the 10 principles that lie behind strong blurbs and 5 common mistakes many people make. After that, I'll go through some case studies and provide a few exercises to help make your book descriptions stronger. Practice doesn't always make perfect, but it does lead to improvement. Finally, I will make the case for seeking outside opinions.

If you want more case studies, free tips, and other perks like discounted blurb rewrites, join the Book Blurb Club by visiting my website: http://www.juliecgilbert.com/

I look forward to working with you, whether solely through this book or directly on your current blurb. Keep on writing. It makes the world wonderful.

Sincerely,

Julie C. Gilbert

Chapter 1:
Blurb Form, Function, and Fashion

Dear Reader,

You may be wondering ...

What is a blurb? (Back Cover Copy/Book Description)

It sounds like something that went wrong in my chemistry class, but in reality, a blurb is the description of a book, movie, or other item. For our purposes, I'm going to confine this definition to books. It goes by several names, but for simplicity, I'm going to stick with blurb. The blurb is meant to draw the customer in, let them know what the book's about, and entice them to go hit that "Add to Cart" button.

How does a blurb differ from a synopsis or an agent query?

Odds are good that if you continue writing, you'll be crafting one or both of those later. How to write each of these tools is a bit beyond the scope of this book, but I want to point out that the principles you learn here will sharpen the type of writing applied in these tools as well.

Quick definitions:
Synopsis: The 1-2 page short form of your book. It introduces each major player and follows the story's twists and turns. 1-2 pages isn't a lot of space when it comes to taking a 80,000-word novel and distilling it down to pertinent plot points and key characters. Choosing the significant pieces of your story for a blurb will help you identify them for the synopsis as well. Presentation is going to differ, but if you can pare down for a blurb, you can definitely do the same

for a synopsis.

Agent query: This is a letter you draft to attract a literary agent. There are giant tomes that detail the "how to" aspect of this particular art form, but understand that although much of it can be a form letter, every agent wants something slightly different in their submission packets. You'll simply have to do the legwork and find out what the agent you're after wishes then go way out of your way to give them everything exactly as they want.

Are blurbs different in fiction and nonfiction?

Short answer: Yes.

Long answer: I deal with more fiction blurbs than nonfiction ones. Their purpose is the same: to attract buyers. That said, I find non-fiction blurbs higher on "selling points" and lower on pretty prose. Part of the attraction of a non-fiction work lies in the functionality of the work. In other words, what can this book teach me about something I already want to know? With fiction, you have roughly 150-250 words to catch a reader's attention. Let's face it, people, attention spans are shrinking at an alarming rate.

What does a great blurb do?

A great blurb grabs a reader's attention and holds it until your entire pitch has been delivered. It should leave them with an "I want more!" gut feeling that can only be assuaged by reading on.

Why do you need to know how to write a blurb?

Your cover should do the heavy lifting of first snagging a reader's attention, but the blurb must then deliver a concise reason as to why that reader should buy your book. You need to let the reader know what they're in for. Odds are good that if you continue with your writing career, you'll need to write some blurbs.

Bonus: Blurbs can be adapted for social media use. Once you've stripped your novel down to its nuts and bolts, modifying the beast to give it Facebook or Twitter legs should be easy.

What does a great blurb look/sound like?

The best blurbs have a flow to them. They may even come across as curt or abrupt in places. You want to instill a mild sense of urgency within the prospective customer. In later chapters, I'll delve more deeply into the form of a great blurb.

Fashion Note: I prefer multiple small paragraphs for ease of reading. I have a friend who wants to keep his blurb down to four paragraphs to keep it "above the fold," but I don't have any hard evidence to support either side. If you can accomplish that easily, go for it, but I wouldn't worry too much about whether you have four or five paragraphs.

One chunky paragraph is slightly intimidating. Massive paragraphs are totally scary. You want to set a mood with the blurb, but "annoyed" is a bad starting point. The exact tone you want may vary with genre, but in general, this is an invitation to step into your world and witness your characters' struggles and triumphs.

Encouragement:

You can do this! Like most things in life, there's a formula to explore. That's what I'm here to teach you. Use it like training wheels. Plug and chug until you're comfortable enough to improvise effectively.

You're a writer. This may or may not be your day job, but it's a skill that will serve you well whether you use it once, twice, or a few hundred times.

Caution: The formula won't immediately solve all of your blurb problems, but it should help. There are certainly times and places to deviate from the formula, but in most cases, it's a matter of molding the pattern to fit your needs. In that sense, it's less a math formula and more of a recipe or a pirate code. (It's more of a guideline.) But I like formulas, so I'm going to continue thinking of it as one.

Chapter 2:
Under Construction – Analysis of Making Blurbs Better

Before we dive too deeply, I'd like to do a quick analysis of some of my early blurbs. It's about time for an overhaul of them anyway. Some of these were written years ago and simply never changed. I'm going to treat them as I would any other client's book description. This involves telling you what I think is right and wrong at the moment and then offering a suggested rewrite.

Ashlynn's Dreams (YA, Science Fiction)

First Draft of *Ashlynn's Dreams*: (Still the one for the Audible version. I should look into changing that.)

Before she was kidnapped, Jillian Marie Antel Blairington was just an average bright, brave, headstrong child. She was excited for life in a new house with her Momma and new Daddy. Afterward, she's all that...and so much more.

Held in a scientific facility, Jillian discovers her past—a family she never knew and a power she doesn't understand. With her ability now activated, she can enter and even shape a person's dreams. Jillian's been kidnapped, and her Gift has been triggered, so she can locate and save Benjamin Connelly, a brother she never even knew she had. She'd better master this strange ability quickly, though, because her life isn't the only one at stake.

Her babysitter, Danielle Matheson, is being held as a hostage to ensure Jillian's full cooperation. Slowly, Jillian begins to learn more about her captor and the other genetically altered children held at the facility. Join Jillian as she tries to survive the training being forced upon her, find her unknown brother, escape with Danielle, and work her way back to a normal life once more.

Comments of First Draft:
First of all, it's way too long for the ebook version, and I need a tagline. Ironically, my second draft is even longer. It does fill out the back of a paperback nicely though. There's something to be said for having two different versions of the blurb, one for paperback and one for ebooks. Most of this book is geared toward making the ebook blurbs better. You probably don't need to know Jillian's full name either. You do need to know Danielle because she's pretty important.

Second Draft:
Twelve-year-old Jillian Blairington is just an ordinary girl— bright, brave, and sometimes a bit too headstrong for her own good. She never thought she was particularly special or different than anybody else.

She was wrong.

Everything changes the day she and her babysitter, Danielle, are kidnapped and taken to a secret scientific facility. There Jillian learns she has a new name, Ashlynn, and a strange connection to the other children at the lab. They each have powerful abilities, Gifts that Jillian doesn't quite understand.

As if that wasn't enough to absorb, Jillian discovers she has a Gift of her own—the power to enter other people's dreams.

Jillian's task seems simple enough: the scientists want her to use her ability to find another Gifted child who has disappeared. But the longer Jillian stays in the facility, the more she realizes that nothing is as it seems ... and everybody has secrets. Besides, the boy's life is not the only one at stake.

The scientists will stop at nothing to force Jillian's cooperation, even if that means threatening Danielle.
Jillian knows they have to get free. But after all they've seen, will they ever truly escape?

Comments of Second Draft:
Once again, this is way too long. I'm pretty sure it still looks nice as a literal back cover copy for a paperback, but for ebooks, there's much trimming required. I still need a tagline. This must have been developed after somebody told me young adult books should declare the main character's age. That's a decent point to keep. I vaguely recall somebody saying the book description gave too much away too. This book is both young adult and science fiction, so I'll need to make some tweaks that reflect those categories.

Suggested Rewrite: (for ebook version)
The kidnapping changes everything ...

Twelve-year-old Jillian Blairington never thought she was particularly special.

She was wrong. She's a Dream Shaper.

The scientists responsible for the genetic modifications kidnap her in order to teach Jillian how to use her Gift. But she isn't alone. They also have her babysitter, Danielle Matheson, snatched to keep her in line.

They also have a task for her.

8

If Jillian can't master her Gift quickly, Danielle might only be the first victim of many.

Comments on the rewrite:
I'm becoming a fan of vague endings. This contains much of the same information as earlier drafts, but it also speeds things along and is way easier to read. I might have to give similar treatments to the others in the series.

Nadia's Tears (YA, Science Fiction)
First Draft of *Nadia's Tears*:
How far would you go to save someone you love?

Having escaped from the scientific facility where her creators trained her to shape dreams, Jillian Blairington thought she was done with them for good. All that changes when her sister, Nadia, suddenly goes silent. Jillian soon discovers that Nadia's in a coma and she—as a Dream Shaper—may be the only one capable of waking her.

Jillian turns to her friend, Danielle Matheson, and together they hatch a crazy plan to get Jillian to Nadia: a second kidnapping. Once by Nadia's side, Jillian must deal with several versions of her sister, including the emotionally wounded Nadie, the fierce Naidine, and the regal Queen Elena.

As she anxiously awaits news from Jillian, Danielle tries to keep a friend from getting into trouble with the wrong crowd. She doesn't realize how quickly things are hurtling from fairly serious to life-threatening.

If Jillian can't solve the mystery of Nadia's coma quickly, she may lose both her sister and her friend.

9

Comments on the First Draft:
I finally have a tagline! It's still a tad on the long side. I don't think I need to name the versions of Nadia. It just confuses things. I do need to keep the reference to Jillian's Gift as a Dream Shaper because that's helping categorize it as a science fiction book.

Suggested Rewrite:
How far would you go to save someone you love?

While learning to use her Dream Shaper Gift, Jillian Blairington met a sister named Nadia who has the power to speak inside one's mind. Jillian's grown rather fond of her.

Now, she's gone silent.

Jillian turns to her friend, Danielle Matheson, and together they hatch a crazy plan to get Jillian to Nadia's side so she can awaken her from the coma.

Meanwhile, Danielle tries to keep a friend out of trouble with human traffickers.

If Jillian can't solve the mystery of Nadia's coma quickly, she may lose both her sister and her friend.

The Collins Case (Christian, Mystery)
First Draft of *The Collins Case*:
Working for the FBI certainly isn't a "normal" job, but Special Agent Julie Ann Davidson has never encountered a case as personal as this one. Although not officially assigned to the case, Ann and her partner, Patrick Duncan, take up the cause of finding Rachel, Jason, and Emily Collins. As if that task wasn't enough, Ann and Patrick also have a baffling case of internet thievery to investigate. Who is Christopher Collins and what about his past is endangering his family? Where are

Rachel and the kids being held? Where is God in the midst of chaos? Will Ann and Patrick arrive in time or will they find only pain?

Comments on First Draft:
Yikes. Ugly paragraph alert. Also, I don't think I need quite so many questions at the end. There are also a ton of names in here. Congrats to me, I think I broke every rule out there. (By the way, my comments to other people aren't quite so bluntly phrased.) I think by now everybody can say it with me: I need a tagline.

Suggested Rewrite:
A young family disappears ...

FBI Special Agent Julie Ann Davidson isn't assigned the case, but she works it anyway because she knows the Collins family. Add in a baffling case of internet thievery, and Ann and her partner, Patrick Duncan, have plenty to think about.

Who took the Collins family and why?

One thing's certain: time is running out.

If Ann and Patrick don't work fast, Rachel Collins and her kids will die.

Comments:
If I stare at this long enough, I'll find more things to tinker with, but it's a workable, much-improved draft. I got daring and name dropped at the end of this. While not usually recommended, I had already used "Collins family" twice in a very short space. Putting in Rachel's name let me give her more of a presence in the blurb and avoid a third mention of "Collins family." When dealing with such tight spaces as we do in blurbs, variety is vital.

Chapter 3:
My Quick and Dirty Method for Blurb Writing

This chapter provides a very quick overview of the elements I put in most blurbs. For perspective, it might help to know that I write mysteries and science fiction. I know the people coming from chapter two are going to be raising their eyebrows at that, but I'm designing this book to be modular. There are people out there who can read things out of order, and I want to be kind to them too. It shocks most of the rest of us. The subsequent chapters will dissect the sections more thoroughly.

1. Tagline:

I'm partial to taglines. These are one-liners that sum up a key aspect or theme of the book. They should be short yet catchy.

Confession: Sometimes, they're even fragments. I know that grates upon our little writer brains, but when it comes to grabbing a reader's attention and keeping it, you can bend the rules a smidge.

2. Introduce the Main Character(s) (MC):

Who is the reader going to meet? What do they do? Why do we care? You don't need to answer all of these questions in the blurb, but you should be able to capture the essence of your main character(s).

Slight Variations:
If you have a main villain and your leading guy/gal, you might want to spend a paragraph on each of them.

Romance stories have two main characters, so you may have to present two paragraphs to introduce them separately.

3. Throw the Monkey Wrench at the MC (Conflict):

What's wrong? Something must not be going right or there wouldn't be a story to tell. I usually use this as a transition to an additional paragraph or as a lead-in to the wrap-up question or statement.

4. Wrap-up Question/Statement (Stakes):

What's going on that the reader should pick up the book to find out if the main character is safe or accomplishes his or her goal? If you want to get cute and it fits the tone of your story, tie the wrap-up line to the title. Stakes might be a separate paragraph from wrap-up, but they definitely should be present in the blurb.

Side note: Those coming from the 5 Steps chapter will notice that this is both Step 4 and Step 5 rolled into one.

Example 1: *Violence in Vegas* (Mystery)
Tagline: Sin City holds some dark secrets ...

Introduction to Main Character: But Marcella Scott's in town to help Angela Melkin-Pierce with a small case of sabotage. Somebody's been slashing guests' tires and ransacking rooms at The Grand Game Hotel. With the guest list including the Reno Birdwatcher's Society and the Paradise Quilting Club, the suspect list is very thin. The only intriguing option is Gatton Technologies, headed by eccentric billionaire, Jeffrey Gatton. When he decides to host a masquerade party at the hotel, Marcella goes undercover.

Monkey Wrench (Conflict): The air of elegance quickly turns to terror when masked men kidnap Gatton and Angela.

Wrap-up (Stakes): Marcella's going to need all of her wits—and a borrowed handgun or two—if she wants to survive the violence in Vegas.

Example 2: *Awakening* (Fantasy)
Tagline: Being the Chosen One could kill her ...

Introduction to Main Character: Victoria Saveron knows two things for certain. Dark forces want to kill her, and her friends have cooler powers than she does. Katrina can shapeshift and Tellen can tap into destructive magic currents.

Transition: Everything else is uncertain and rumors abound.

Monkey Wrench (Conflict): Victoria might be the Chosen One, whatever that means. Her father might be able to help them, but only if they can find him. Coldhaven's villagers might be able to offer them food and shelter. Some fool might be running around unlocking Darkland portals to raise an undead army.

Wrap-up (Stakes): The further Victoria and her companions get on their journey, the more dangers and betrayals they face. They must awaken Vic's true powers or forfeit the world.

Example 3: *The Dark Side of Science*
(Science fiction)
Tagline: The mind can hold powerful secrets.

Introduction to Main Character: When Dr. Jessica Paladon worked for her friend, Dr. Dean Devya, she helped create Nadia, one of the world's few Minders. Tough circumstances drove her away from that life, and to protect the secrets, she willingly took a drug that induced amnesia.

Transition: But now she needs those memories.

Monkey Wrench (Conflict): Two children—her children—Nadia and Varick are competing in a winners-take-all, losers-might-die competition for the biggest secret government contract out there. They're fighting for the right to exist.

Wrap-up (Stakes): If Jessie can't remember, how will she help them survive?

Chapter 4:
10 Principles to Crafting Dream Blurbs

Overview:
You're probably thinking "10 principles, 5 mistakes, 5 steps" get to the point, lady. I'm confining the principles to their own section because they're not always apparent in the final product. These are the rules and reminders that will put you on the right track.

Keep your eye on the target: the reader buys your book. You need to strike that fine balance between enticing them and overwhelming them.

10 Principles of Writing Great Blurbs:
Principle #1: Generate a Great Tagline
The tagline must capture the reader's attention and intrigue them enough to continue reading. This statement or question should be short and snappy. It's an appetizer, not a meal.

Example taglines:
Malia's Miracles (YA science fiction): How much is one life worth?
Varick's Quest (YA science fiction): Genetically altering humans is illegal ...
The Kiverson Case (Christian mystery): One man's vendetta could cost them everything ...

Principle #2: Know Your Selling Points
What are the 3-5 points the reader should know about your book?

What makes your story awesome? You've poured hours of your life into creating these people, places, and events. You love them, but you have to leave some of them out of the blurb. Is the book light-hearted and fun, dark and gritty, deep and powerful? What do you seek to do with the book? Do you want to entertain people, make them think, show them a common flaw in mankind, or some combination thereof?

Principle #3: Know Your Secrets
These are the things you will hold back from the reader. What would you consider a spoiler? These things are still important because they will influence the mood you're setting.

Principle #4: Know Your Team
Making cuts is difficult, but you need to focus on the main character(s). Somebody asked about a cast of characters. In other words, what if everybody's important? In that case, you should probably focus on the group as a whole. What binds them together and defines them?

Principle #5: Know Your Audience and Genre
You should already know this from writing your book. Are you targeting middle grade students, young adults, adults only, a mix, men only, middle aged women, or some other group? The audience and genre will help shape the language you use in your blurb. This might affect some word choices.

Principle #6: Set the Correct Tone
You should set a tone that matches your book or go for a neutral, engaging vibe in your blurb. Once again, word choice will be affected by your tone.

Principle #7: Tell a Miniature Story
Blurbs are bigger than elevator pitches yet smaller than synopses. You need a hook. We're calling that the tagline. You also need to answer some questions. Who's involved in the story? What's going on? Where/when does this story take

place? What problems face the protagonists? Why should the reader care about these people?

Principle #8: Establish the Stakes

You can't escape conflict. In fact, you need it to keep the story going. If there's no conflict, there's no story. It may sound harsh, but it's true. Conflict drives plots forward, challenge characters, and makes stories memorable.

Principle #9: Instill a Sense of Urgency

Blurbs are sales pitches, but there's no reason it should sound like you want to sell them something. Regardless of genre, you need the reader to want to order your book and immediately dive into it.

Principle #10: Dance with the Words – The Importance of Word Choice

This might sound akin to saying "find the magic and insert here." Essentially, you need to try different combinations of words. Word choice rears its important head again. The English language has many words, so try to use a variety of them. Most words carry their own context. Some are naturally lighter or heavier than others. Take this little section for example. The word "dance" is light, airy, and springy.

Consider some other words that might have been used: play, toy, manipulate, control, rig, experiment, try, and test. "Play with the words" would also have worked for my meaning but it's slightly less fun than dance. I mean for you to "toy" with and "manipulate" the words, but both have negative leanings. "Control" and "rig" have the same problem. You are carefully controlling each word you choose to put in your blurb, but stating it that way seems overbearing and oppressive. "Experiment," "try," and "test" would also work for my meaning, but they seem clinical, cold, and lifeless.

Chapter 5:
5 Common Mistakes to Avoid

Although I'm only going to present the mistakes here, I will try to point them out in the case studies.

Here's the full list:
Mistake #1: Telling too Much – Giving Away Secrets
Mistake #2: Rambling on Forever – Wasting Words on Unnecessary Things
Mistake #3: Gigantic Paragraphs
Mistake #4: Name Dumping
Mistake #5: Cryptic Teasers
Bonus Mistake #1: Changing Tenses
Bonus Mistake #2: Being Vague

Mistake #1: Telling too Much – Giving Away Secrets
A blurb is not a synopsis. It should not give away every major twist to the story. You want to get the reader to buy the book, not tell them the whole story. Keep some secrets! At its heart, the blurb is an invitation to open the book and read more.

Mistake #2: Rambling on Forever – Wasting Words on Unnecessary Things
This might be a personal preference, but I don't like long book descriptions. That might seem hypocritical given some of the blurbs I've written in the past, but long blurbs run the risk of rambling. (And whether Amazon really wants to change my descriptions or not, I have updated most of them.) Telling too much and rambling may sound like the same thing, but I define the first in terms of giving away plot points and the second as unnecessarily defining stuff that should be obvious. I've definitely fallen prey to asking too many questions at the end of a blurb. (See *The Collins Case* blurb if

you want to view this mistake in all its glory.)

Mistake #3: Gigantic Paragraphs

I don't think there's any set rule of "thou shalt not use more than __ words per paragraph." However, paragraphs exist to ease readability. Use them wisely. If you want something to stand out, give that part its own paragraph. Someone once told me that short sentences lend themselves more readily to suspense. Whether you're writing a mystery or not, it's a good thing to keep in mind for blurbs because you do want to create a situation where the reader is in suspense. You also want to make the blurb easy to read. Multiple small paragraphs are easier to read than gigantic ones.

Mistake #4: Name Dumping

Don't waste the words telling us everybody's name. Try to keep the name dropping to a minimum. 2-3 people is usually enough. Romance probably has 2 focal points. Mystery usually has 1-2 points, hero and villain.

This one can be especially deadly to fantasy and science fiction blurbs. It's difficult to decide which people, place, and object names to include. Likely, you've done a lot of world-building you're proud of in your 125000-word fantasy novel. But this ain't your glossary. We need to know who's who and what's what in a very tight space.

Name Aside (Rant): I probably have way more to say than you'd ever want to hear about names. It's kind of an obsession of mine, especially in fantasy and science fiction. My biggest irritant when it comes to names is something I can't pronounce to save my dear life. I know there are six-figure fantasy authors out there who use most of the letters in the English language in every elven city they create, but most of us will never be them anyway. There are other aspects of their writing to emulate. Unpronounceable names is not one of them.

Mistake #5: Cryptic Teasers

This one's tricky. While you do want to leave them with a sense of longing, you do not want to confuse the reader! Think: "hmm, that's interesting, what's next?" not "huh?"

Bonus Mistake #1: Changing Tenses

Don't change tenses. I've seen a few blurbs written in first person with a shift to third near the end. Most blurbs are best done in the third person. There are always exceptions, and I know some have been written in first person to good effect. However, while a first person perspective can get you very close to the main character, recall the main job of the blurb. It's supposed to be about the book as a whole.

Bonus Mistake #2: Being Vague

Try to avoid telling the reader absolutely nothing. This is close to cryptic teasers but more distinct. There are times to keep a blurb short, but a line that's so general that it doesn't say much of anything, doesn't help a reader choose that "buy me" button.

Note: You're competing with hundreds of thousands of books, even if you list your book for free. Make the presentation as crisp and clear as you can.

Chapter 6:
10⁺ Case Studies in Making Blurbs Shine

Each case study is used with the author's permission. Each case study is used with the author's permission. For your convenience, I'll go through and add to my initial comments to tell you which of the common mistakes or bonus mistakes I think the blurb is making.

If you really want to jump in to the blurb writing process, move to Chapter 7. However, I've placed this lengthy chapter here because I think it's useful to see what could be better and what already works before leaping into actual blurb creation.

Caution: author notes may contain spoilers for their stories. I have modified some of them slightly for the sake of clarity. My comments (and author comments) aren't always phrased in grammatically correct ways.

(It might look a wee bit strange, but I'm putting in page breaks to start case studies on a new page.)

Here's the full list again (in case you're skipping around):
Mistake #1: Telling too Much – Giving Away Secrets
Mistake #2: Rambling on Forever – Wasting Words on Unnecessary Things
Mistake #3: Gigantic Paragraphs
Mistake #4: Name Dumping
Mistake #5: Cryptic Teasers
Bonus Mistake #1: Changing Tenses
Bonus Mistake #2: Being Vague

Case Study #1: *Surprises*

Title: *Surprises*
Author: Amy Allen
Genre: Paranormal Romance

Side Note: I usually like to work with a blurb the author has already written, but in this case, I took some notes she gave me and a single-sentence stab at a blurb and expanded from there.

Author Notes:

Surprises is the prequel to *Second Chances* and is John and Brandi's story. John and Brandi have known each other since 1848 and were together off and on from 1870 until 1998 (She moved to Denver and in with him in 2000). She is like she is in *Second Chances*—immortal from birth, a vampire and he is semi-mortal (not vampire or shifter or anything) so he has been alive since 1834 and unless something catastrophic happens (which did to kill him in 2004) he will live until he chooses to die). So anyway—he is surprising her by asking her to marry him, she surprises him with finding out she's pregnant—with triplets.

Original Blurb:

John, taking everyone by surprise with a single question, and getting his own surprise or two.

My Comments:
You need a tagline.

As previously mentioned, it's not really the full blurb. I've worked with this author before, and she trusted that I'd write a blurb for her. Even so, if this were the blurb, it'd fall under "being vague."

Suggested Rewrite for *Surprises*:
Forever is a long time.

For John, life will go on until he chooses to die—or something catastrophic happens. For Brandi, a vampire, life could stretch on forever.

They've been together on and off since 1870, but he's finally ready to ask an important question. Little does he know, she also has a few surprises hidden inside.

Life's full of surprises, but will their relationship last with these new twists?

Final Version (from Amazon or directly from the author):
Forever is a long time.

For John, life will go on until he chooses to die—or something catastrophic happens.
For Brandi, a vampire, life could stretch on forever.

They've been together on and off since 1870, but he's finally ready to ask an important question. Little does he know, she also has a few surprises hidden inside.

Life's full of surprises, but will their relationship last with these new twists?

Additional Commentary:
Sometimes, the author will choose to go with my version of the blurb. That's gratifying, but not necessary as you'll see shortly.

Aside: I just learned that you could make certain text bold in Amazon's Author Central site. But be warned, it does some funky things with spacing, like randomly deciding you don't need certain spaces. Still, it might be worth the irritation to be able to bold your tagline.

Case Study #2: *KAPU*

Title: *KAPU*
Author: Dave Schoonover
Genre: Mystery

Original Blurb:
Maui Detective Lei Texeira has her hands full: someone is murdering the developers of a proposed resort that has the Native Hawaiian community up in arms, and Lei's best resource might be her challenging young investigator.

Katie McHenry is a new officer in the MPD, assigned to Lei's team. She has the mind of a hacker, a black belt in karate, and an attitude that Lei recognizes: the bad guys don't follow the rules, so why should she?

When the killer starts posting taunting messages on the internet, Katie may be the key to solving the case before anyone else dies.

My Comments:
You need a tagline.

Updated Comments: Although this doesn't ramble on forever, there are a few sections I think use more words than necessary. For example, the part that talks about the attitude Lei recognizes. It would probably be stronger if it simply said "… and a dangerous attitude" then ended that sentence and explained the attitude in a separate sentence. Also, there are some passive verbs here that might be strengthened. Especially in a mystery blurb, it's imperative to keep it sharp.

29

Suggested Rewrite for *KAPU*:
Nature. Nurture. Preserve. Protect. Murder?

The (company name) wants to build (resort name) at (location), (description of location... for example, a historical site ... home to some type of rare animal?). The situation creates high tension with the Native Hawaiian community, but somebody's taking the feud one giant step further by killing off (company name...board members?).

Maui Detective Leilani Texeira has her hands full with solving the politically charged case and mentoring MPD's hotshot rookie, Katie McHenry. The young officer has the mind of a hacker, a black belt in karate, and a dangerous attitude. *Bad guys don't follow rules, why should I?* Lei can sympathize with Katie's outlook, but she is also responsible for keeping the kid alive.

The killer also has a bad attitude: *You can't catch me or stop me. Can you guess who's going down next?* And he or she is more than willing to taunt the police. In this high tech, high stakes game of wits, Katie might hold the key to solving the case, if she lives long enough to tell the tale.

Final Version (from Amazon or directly from the author):

Kapu means forbidden. Desecration means death. This ancient Hawaiian legal system collapsed in the early 19th century—or did it?

Kuleana Development wants to build a high-end resort in Maui's historic and sacred 'Iao Valley.' Their plan angers the Native Hawaiian and environmental communities, who have joined forces to stop it.

But when someone raises the stakes and starts killing off the development team, Maui Police Detective Leilani Texeira is on the hunt. She has her hands full, between solving the politically-charged case and mentoring MPD's hotshot rookie, Katie McHenry.

The young officer has the mind of a hacker, a black belt in karate, and a dangerous attitude: *Bad guys don't follow the rules, so why should she?* Lei can understand Katie's outlook, but she is also responsible for keeping the kid alive.

The killer has a dangerous attitude too, combining cold-blooded murder with a willingness to taunt the police via the internet. In this high tech, high stakes game of wits, Katie might hold the key to solving the case—if she lives long enough.

Additional Commentary:
As you can see, not every author takes what I've written and slaps it up on Amazon. Even if you decide to hire me or somebody else to give your blurb a fresh jolt of energy, it's still your story. You get to make the final call on what stays and what goes. You want to make the blurb your own. At the same time, you can see that the final contains some of my suggestions and is stronger than the original draft.

Oddly, the blurb got longer as we went through this process. That is definitely rare.

Case Study #3: *Holly and Mr. Ivy*

Title: *Holly and Mr. Ivy*
Author: Jessica L. Elliott
Genre: Contemporary Romance; subgenre – animal heroes

Author Notes:

This is the info for Holly and Mr. Ivy. It's a contemporary, sweet romance which takes place at Christmastime. The main characters include two shelter dogs Holly and Kip, who can speak to each other but not to the humans in the story, their owner Tremayne Ivy, and Victoria Claremont. Tremayne is an English teacher at the local high school where Victoria is a math teacher and recently took the coaching position Tremayne wanted, sparking an intense rivalry. If you need/want more info on the book, let me know.

Original Blurb:

You know those stories where a pet accidentally sets up the romance?

It wasn't an accident.

Canine matchmaker Holly has been given her first assignment and it's a doozy. She must help her human find the perfect mate. The only problem is he is absolutely not interested in the woman Holly and her assistant, Kip, find for him. In fact, Tremayne Ivy and Victoria Claremont can't stand each other. It will take all Holly's training and a little Christmas magic to take these rivals from completely at odds to walking down the aisle.

My Comments:

Tagline could be shorter, snappier. What are the stakes? What happens if this doesn't work out? Does your canine heroine have a motto for her business? What are the stakes for Holly? For the people? Who is her human? Ivy? Okay, Ivy owns Holly, but Kip? Does Kip belong to Claremont? (The relationships aren't clear here. I have a better idea because of your notes.)

Overall, it's not a bad blurb. It's a little wordy in places. It also drops a lot of names in a very tight space.

Suggested Rewrite for *Holly and Mr. Ivy*:

Pets can't accidentally spark romance ...

But they can be matchmakers.

Meet Holly. She's an adorable (dog species mix here) on a mission to find the perfect mate for her human. Unfortunately, Holly's human project just lost the coveted (job title) coaching job to the lovely lady she wants to pair him with.

It will take all of Holly's skill and a little Christmas magic to turn the rivals into lifelong lovers.

Here are some other taglines to consider:

Each would start the blurb with a slightly diff tone.

Alt tag 1: First assignments bite. (Only use if this fits your story! I don't know the tone so I can't say if it fits.)

Alt tag 2: Holly's first matchmaker assignment is a doozy. (It's tamer but it also doesn't take risks.)

Alt tag 3: Holly's got one chance to become a matchmaker ...

And the first assignment is impossible.

Additional Commentary:
Last I checked, the old blurb is still up there on Amazon. That's cool. Nobody is obligated to take the suggested rewrite. I've made my case for the changes I offered, but it's the author's prerogative to accept or reject the suggestions.

Aside on Rejecting Suggestions:
I did this one for free to practice the genre. People who understand the value of the work take the suggestions to heart more often because they're more invested in it. There is truth in perceived value. Gee, maybe I should charge more. Some people have the complete opposite reaction and agonize over it more because they feel guilty not liking something somebody took the time to do for free. Let me clarify. I don't mean you're not emotionally invested in your work. That's probably exactly what's standing between you accepting and rejecting suggestions.

I'll reiterate some of these points later, but I want to take a moment to discuss a few of the possible reasons people might not like the blurb suggestions:
1) It's way off the mark. This could be your fault or mine. The original blurb and notes you've given me could be misleading. Obviously, it helps if I've read the entire work, but in a rewrite, the odds of that having been the case are slim.

2) You're too attached to the way you've worded things. Without naming names or situations, I'll say that I've worked with people who REALLY wanted to say something a particular way that I felt was awkward. They'd paid me for my opinion, so I'd told them in the comments that it sounded odd to me. End of the day, it's your story blurb and you do what you want with it. Still, try to remember the blurb's not for you. It's for the public.

35

3) You really like the style of your initial blurb. In my experience, the people with the most style in their blurbs often reject suggestions with a greater frequency than other clients. As a writer, style's a great thing. It's what takes the words we write and makes them shine as a story. You want the blurb to reflect your tone, but you don't need it to sound exactly like the book itself. The blurb is a specific marketing tool, and therefore, there are some conventions to follow most of the time.

Case Study #4: *Born to Love*

Title: *Born to Love (A Keiki and Lia Thriller)*
Author: Amy Shojai
Genre: Thriller

Original Blurb:
A GIRL seeks her past to find her future.
A WARRIOR gambles his sacrifice will point the way home.
A PUPPY finds her true purpose--when she learns to love.

At four months old, a puppy's job is to learn and Keiki relishes the sights, sounds and smells of her world. But people often leave her confused and frustrated, especially when humans control all the really good stuff like treats, toys and games.

Lia Corazon has "the touch," a connectedness with animals inherited from a mother she never knew. Estranged from her family, Lia channels her energy—and emotion—into the dogs she trains in her North Texas kennel. Lia delights in Keiki's eagerness to learn, but becomes uneasy when there's something "off" about the new owner.

A raging storm, violent flood, and scary creatures threaten Keiki's life, until her Rottweiler bravery comes through--with a little help from a mysterious canine warrior. But what can a good-dog do when the enemy is human? How can Keiki-pup save Lia from a violent, raging killer?

My Comments:

I would take out at least the middle tagline because you don't have anything about the warrior until the very end, and there, it's sort of a side note. I'd also try to combine the first two taglines into one. Having three taglines slows things down. Sentiments in the rest are good, though I'd tighten the wording to get to the punch quicker. The new owner thing is confusing ... is it referring to the owner of the dog or the owner of the kennel? You say her kennel but it's not completely clear. "Raging" is repeated.

This blurb contains too much information.

Suggested Rewrite for *Born to Love*:

Can the past unlock the future and love preserve a life?

A puppy's job is to learn. Keiki relishes the sights, sounds, and smells of the world, but people frustrate and confuse her. Why do humans control all the good stuff?

Lia Corazon channels her energy and emotions into the dogs she trains in her North Texas kennel. She especially enjoys the four-month-old Rottweiler's enthusiasm, but the pup's owner makes her uneasy. There's something very ... wrong about him.

Keiki must face both violent weather and unpredictable people if she's to save Lia from a killer.

Final Version:
Can the past unlock the future and love preserve a life?

A puppy's job is to learn. Keiki relishes the sights, sounds and smells of her world, but people frustrate and confuse her. Why do humans control all the good stuff?

Lia Corazon channels her energy and emotions into the dogs she trains in her North Texas kennel. She especially enjoys four-month-old Keiki's enthusiasm, but the pup's owner makes her uneasy. There's something very...wrong about him.

When a vicious storm, violent flood, and scary creatures menace Keiki, her Rottweiler bravery comes through. But what can a good-dog do when a human enemy threatens? Keiki must use all she's learned if she's to save Lia from a killer.

Additional Commentary:
This author kept most of my suggestions, but once again, she made some subtle and very powerful changes to the final version. This is great. That's what should happen. While having an outsider's perspective can help in the initial shaping process, it's also advisable to take the fledgling blurb and make it your own.

Case Study #5: *All the Way My Savior Leads*

Title: *All the Way My Savior Leads*
Author: Faith Blum
Genre: Christian Western

Original Blurb by Faith Blum:
I looked around. "Anybody else hungry?"
"I am!" Jeremiah exclaimed from the doorway.
I grinned. "You're always hungry."
He stuck his tongue out at me. "Am not."
Raised an eyebrow. "Tell me one time you weren't."
Jeremiah paused. He opened and shut his mouth three times. "Then again, you may be right."

Henry and Caroline's parents die and the pair are dumped in a faraway orphanage. At least the two have each other. Three years later, Henry is almost 18 and knows he will soon be forced to leave the place he's called home for three years, and worse, his younger sister.

Plotting villains and overly generous offers complicate Henry's decision. Does he leave her in the relative safety of the orphanage, or risk it all on his dream of farming? He asks God for help, but with no clear sign, Henry's left to trust his faith and his God.

My Comments:
The excerpt in the beginning is interesting but confusing. There's no mention of who "I" is and there's no mention of Jeremiah in the rest of the blurb. Keep the focus on Henry and his sister. Given the end, I'd keep the focus on Henry alone … since the rest revolves around his decision.

The blurb also moves from "the pair" to Henry alone. While not a shift in tense, it has almost the same jarring effect.

Suggested Rewrite for *All the Way My Savior Leads*:
Tragedy stole everything from him … except her …

Three years ago, a (what happened to the parents? Tragic accident? Brutal murder?) orphaned Henry and Caroline (last name?). The harsh years at the poorly run (orphanage name) have forged a strong bond between the pair.

But Henry's about to age out.

He must choose whether to leave his only family behind in relative safety, or take her with him as he pursues dreams of owning a farm. Henry trusts that God has a plan for him, but little does he know that others have plans for him and his little sister as well. He will need all his faith to find the right path.

41

Final Version by Faith Blum:
Caroline and I walked out the back door and went into the barn.
"What are we going to do?" Caroline asked.
"Head out on our own. Saddle Whitey, please."
Caroline's mouth gaped open. "They'll find us."
"I know."
Caroline sighed. "What can we do then?"
I shook my head. "We can stick together. Always."

Tragedy stole everything from him … except her …

Three years ago, an illness orphaned Henry and Caroline Salisbury. The harsh years at the orphanage have forged a strong bond between the pair.

But Henry's about to age out.

He must choose whether to leave his only family behind in relative safety, or take her with him as he pursues dreams of owning a farm. Henry trusts that God has a plan for him, but little does he know that others have plans for him and his younger sister as well. He will need all his faith to find the right path.

Additional Commentary:
The author accepted most of my suggestions but added her own flair. I'd asked her in an email why the quote and apparently it's just something she's done for all her books. That's a good mark for branding, but I suggested she pick a new passage that focused on the siblings. The new excerpt pairs with the blurb nicely.

Case Study #6: *Joss the Seven*

Title: Joss the Seven
Author: J. Philip Horne
Genre: YA Fantasy

Author Note:
I have several blurbs I use for different contexts, but the last one is the main one on Amazon.

Short (29 words, 148 characters)
14-year-old Joss has superpowers, and that's a problem! A criminal gang wants to force him into a life of crime, and Joss is running out of options.

Suggested Rewrite:
Joss Morgan's new superpowers attract all sorts of attention, even criminals.

Short (17 words, 92 characters)
14-year-old Joss Morgan just found out he has superpowers, and that's a super-sized problem!

Suggested Rewrite:
Joss Morgan has superpowers. Big powers, big problems!

Short (16 words, 81 characters)
14-year-old Joss Morgan just found out he has superpowers. It may get him killed.

Suggested Rewrite:
Joss Morgan's new superpowers might just get him killed.

Medium (69 words, 350 characters)
14yo Joss Morgan loves a good prank, but the joke's on him when he discovers he has superpowers. The Mockers are coming for Joss, and he doesn't know why. When they show

up at his house, Joss is out of time. He sets up a desperate, high-stakes prank to save his family. If he fails, he won't end up in the principal's office. He'll be six feet under.

Original Blurb by J. Philip Horne:
Fourteen-year-old Joss Morgan loves a good prank, but the joke's on him when he discovers he has superpowers. He quickly learns that with the new powers comes real danger. The Mockers are coming for Joss, and he doesn't know why, or even who they really are.

The Guild of Sevens sends Mara to train Joss in his new powers, and she uses him to fight back against the Mockers. But nothing adds up, and pretty soon Joss is wondering which side he's working for.

When the Mockers arrive at his home, Joss is out of time. He sets up a high-stakes prank to save his family. This time he knows that if he fails, he won't end up in the principal's office; he'll be six feet under.

Comments:
Do we need to know he's 14? You need a tagline. Parts of this are wordy. What happens that "nothing's adding up"? What kind of pranks does he pull? Why do we need to know he is a prankster? What kind of prank can he pull to save his family? Who is his family? (Mom, Dad, siblings?) With it left this vague, we don't get a real feel for the stakes. You might want to leave out the Mocker's name. What are his super powers? Mention of the principal's office needs to happen sooner if you want to keep it in the later part.

This blurb is okay, but there are too many names. For example, Guild of Sevens, Mara, and Mockers are all people and entities we'll read about if we buy the book, but having them named clutters the blurb.

Note: The author answered that it's a convention with young adult and middle grade books to put the age of the character since the target audience tends to be 1-2 years younger than the main character.

Suggested Rewrite for *Joss the Seven*:

New powers. New problems.

Joss Morgan loves playing pranks, but it's no joke that he has superpowers. Those powers come with real danger.

Heroes and criminals want Joss to join them. Both will use him.

His life isn't the only one on the line.

If Joss can't figure out who to trust, his whole family could die.

Final from Amazon by J. Philip Horne:

New powers. New problems.

14-year-old Joss Morgan loves joking around, but it's no joke when he discovers he has superpowers. Those powers come with real danger. Heroes and criminals want Joss to join them. Both will use him. Everyone has secrets. And his life isn't the only one on the line. If Joss can't figure out who to trust, his whole family could die.

Additional Commentary:

I like that the author was able to make the tagline bold text. It adds a nice touch. He wanted less paragraphs so decided to move some of the words around. That's fine. I hope it helps him reach more people. I also liked how the author offered a few different versions because that's also important in things like social media presence.

Side Note: The author sent me some data from some Amazon ads that show that the clicks per sale and cost per sale are better than some of his past ads with older versions of the blurb. That's a great sign.

Case Study #7: *Memoirs of a Girl Who Loves God*

Title: *Memoirs of a Girl Who Loves God*
Author: C.L. Wells
Genre: YA Christian Fiction

Original by C.L. Wells:

Fourteen-year-old Krystal finds herself flailing when her parents separate. Withdrawing from her family and friends, she begins cutting. No one knows.

At her new school, she makes one single friend, Em, who invites her to volunteer at the local homeless shelter. There, Krystal discovers fellow misfits, including Brandon, a boy from her school. How can Krystal start a new life when the scars of her old one will never fully heal?

Author Notes:

This (original blurb) seems more of a summarization than anything else. Self-harm is a must mention because people tend to get upset if you don't and they didn't know.

I'm also not thrilled with using "misfits" in the blurb. While I do use it in the book, it takes on a different meaning from someone who hasn't read it yet.

Thanks for taking a peek!

Comments:

You need a tagline. Do we need to know she's 14? Yes, this sounds like a summary. I like the end question. It's got a lot of mentions of her name for such a short blurb. Agreed, "misfits" isn't the best word here. It conjures the wrong image.

There are also too many other names for such a tiny blurb.

Suggested Rewrite for *Memoirs of a Girl Who Loves God*:
Silent pain. Secret Scars.

When her parents divorce (separate??), Krystal (last name?) finds herself flailing. She withdraws from family and friends and begins cutting because it gives her a sense of control.

No one knows her pain.

Now living only with Mom (Dad??), Krystal lands in a new school where she makes a single friend, Em. Together, they volunteer at a homeless shelter and work with (?? disenfranchised people??, troubled teens??).

How will Krystal help others when her hidden scars still sting?

(Given additional notes by author.)
Suggested Rewrite Draft 2:
Silent pain. Secret Scars.

When her parents divorce, Krystal (last name?) finds herself flailing. She withdraws from family and friends and begins cutting because it gives her a sense of control.

No one knows her pain.

Now living only with Mom, Krystal lands in a new school where she makes a single friend, Em. Together, they volunteer at a homeless shelter, serving soup and working alongside a whole host of different people. (1 sentence about the type of people she meets and works with. Hint at their troubles.)

Everybody has their secrets, but will anybody understand? How will Krystal help others when her hidden scars still sting?

Final by C.L. Wells:
Silent pain. Secret Scars.

When her parents divorce, Krystal finds herself flailing. She withdraws from family and friends and begins cutting because it's the one thing she can control.

No one knows her pain.

Now living only with Mom, Krystal lands in a new school where she makes a single friend, Em. Together, they volunteer at a homeless shelter, serving soup and working alongside a diverse group with a few eccentrics sprinkled in.

Everyone has secrets, but who will understand hers? How will Krystal help others when her hidden scars still sting?

Additional Commentary:
Once again, you can see that the author is able to take my suggestions and make it even better because she knows her story. "Eccentrics" is a great substitution for "misfits."

Author Endorsement:
"My fiction story covers a sensitive topic that people tend to shy away from. An excellent cover and blurb are as just as essential to selling your work as your skill, if not more so. I'd done my best with the blurb and even got help from author friends, but still found it lacking. Julie's changes offered a fresh take with an awesome tagline to boot. She's easy to work with and offered solid advice at a very reasonable rate."
~ C.L. Wells, *Memoirs of a Girl Who Loves God*

Case Study #8-10: *A Snake in Paradise, Seal of a Monk,* and *Charade at Sea*

Title: *A Snake in Paradise, Seal of a Monk,* and *Charade at Sea*
Author: Eden Baylee
Genre: Mystery/thriller

Original by Eden Baylee (A Snake in Paradise):
Lainey Lee has always dreamed of going to Hawaii. It should have been her honeymoon trip, only it never happened. Now, in a poetic twist of fate, she is making the journey twenty-seven years later—following a messy divorce.

Once on the Big Island, Lainey discovers paradise, but white sand beaches and blue skies are not all Hawaii has to offer. She soon meets Julian, a mysterious stranger ten years her junior. They share an instant connection.

Lainey is eager to shed the fears that trapped her in a loveless marriage, but is Julian a tempting distraction, a new beginning, or a snake in paradise?

Comments:
I think we need more tagline here. Yeah, I think with a little reworking, we can make it stronger.

The paragraphs are on the long side.

Suggested Rewrite:
Hawaii offers white sand beaches, blue skies, and other beautiful mysteries ...

But paradise can also harbor danger.

Lainey Lee always dreamed of going to Hawaii. It was the honeymoon trip that never happened. Now, post-messy divorce, a poetic twist of fate takes her to the Big Island. Soon, she meets a mysterious stranger ten years her junior.

She's eager to shed the fears that trapped her in a loveless marriage. But is Julian a tempting distraction, a new beginning, or a snake in paradise?

Final from Amazon by Eden Baylee:
Lainey Lee has always dreamed of going to Hawaii. It should have been her honeymoon trip, only it never happened. Now, in a poetic twist of fate, she is making the journey twenty-seven years later—following a messy divorce.

Once on the Big Island, Lainey discovers paradise, but white sand beaches and blue skies are not all Hawaii has to offer. She soon meets Julian, a mysterious stranger ten years her junior. They share an instant connection.

Lainey is eager to shed the fears that trapped her in a loveless marriage, but is Julian a tempting distraction, a new beginning, or a snake in paradise?

Additional Commentary:
The author stuck with her original blurb, and that's fine. It's a great blurb. I still think it would be stronger with some sort of tagline, but the book doesn't seem to have suffered any from not having one. It's a rarity that my suggested rewrite is longer than the original. Typically, I am chopping off words left and right to pare things down. Here, I wanted to expand

a little so the picture of paradise comes through more clearly.

Original by Eden Baylee (Seal of a Monk):
The ancient jungles of Kauai provide the perfect setting for self-discovery.

Despite the terror she experienced on her last trip, Lainey Lee returns to Hawaii to manage a silent meditation course on the Coconut Coast. Twenty-five women are under her care for ten days in a beautiful and remote location. Lainey expects to find inner peace, but four days into the course, one of the meditators disappears without a trace.

Did the girl leave of her own free will, or was she lured away by a strange cult? Lainey is frantic to answer these questions. As her desperation grows, she finds help from an unexpected source—a retired Navy SEAL named Maximillian Scott.

Now, Lainey has two mysteries to solve: what happened to the missing girl and the case of her own heart. Can she ever trust a man again?

Suggested Rewrite:
Kauai's ancient jungles are the perfect place for self-discovery.

Despite a harrowing first experience, Lainey Lee returns to Hawaii to manage a silent meditation course on the Coconut Coast. For ten days, she'll oversee twenty-five women seeking inner peace.
That's the plan until one of the meditators disappears.

Did she leave of her own free will, or was she lured away by a strange cult. Lainey's frantic to find answers, and as her desperation grows, she discovers unexpected help in the form of ex-Navy SEAL Maximillian Scott.

Now, Lainey has two mysteries to unravel: where is the missing girl and can she ever trust a man again?

Final from Amazon by Eden Baylee:
The ancient jungles of Kauai provide the perfect setting for self-discovery.

Despite the terror she experienced on her last trip, Lainey Lee returns to Hawaii to manage a silent meditation course on the Coconut Coast. Twenty-five women are under her care for ten days in a beautiful and remote location. Lainey expects to find inner peace, but four days into the course, one of the meditators disappears without a trace.

Did the girl leave of her own free will, or was she lured away by a strange cult? Lainey is frantic to answer these questions. As her desperation grows, she finds help from an unexpected source—a retired Navy SEAL named Maximillian Scott.

Now, Lainey has two mysteries to solve: what happened to the missing girl and the case of her own heart. Can she ever trust a man again?

Additional Comments:
I still think the author's trying to do too much in this blurb, but it's still got a flow that lends itself nicely to mystery. The book description lets the reader know what they're in for without delving into spoiler territory.

Original by Eden Baylee (Charade at Sea, book 3):
A luxury cruise of Hawaii is ideal for a budding romance, or is it?

Lainey Lee accepts an invitation from ex-Navy SEAL Max Scott to cruise around the Hawaiian Islands. Having shared an incredible experience the first time they met in Kauai, she is eager to learn if they have enough in common for a future together.

While on the luxury ship, Lainey meets Clara Simmons, a fifty-something newlywed who is on her honeymoon. Clara confesses her husband, Robert, is much younger than her and involved in secret missions around the world. Lainey is intrigued.

When the opportunity arises to meet him, she and Max invite the couple for a formal evening with the ship's Captain. Lainey takes an instant disliking to Robert, but she ignores her intuition. Unbeknownst to her, Max also has his suspicions.

As her feelings for Max grow, Lainey can't help but wonder what kind of a charade is being played at sea.

Comments:
Not sure you need quite so many names. If the focus is on Max and Lainey, let it rest mainly with them. Looks pretty good, some of your emphasis could be different though. The last sentence keeps with your previous blurbs ... which is good. But I think it should be a question like the others.

Shorten tagline? You mention HI a few seconds later. It seems like a lot of detail (sorta getting into synopsis territory).

Suggested Rewrite:
A luxury cruise is ideal for a budding romance … or is it?

Lainey Lee and ex-Navy SEAL, Max Scott, had an incredible experience when they met in Kauai. A romantic cruise around the Hawaiian Islands is the perfect way to explore the possibility of becoming more than friends.

But mystery abounds.

Lainey meets a lovely fifty-something newlywed on her honeymoon. The chatty lady has nothing but good things to say about the man, but Lainey and Max both get bad vibes from him.

Do they have time to fall in love and survive the charade being played at sea?

Final from Amazon by Eden Baylee:
A luxury cruise is ideal for a budding romance … or is it?

Lainey Lee and ex-Navy SEAL, Max Scott, shared an incredible experience when they met in Kauai. A romantic cruise around the Hawaiian Islands seems perfect for discovering if they can become more than just friends.

But mystery abounds.

Lainey meets a fifty-something newlywed on her honeymoon. The chatty woman speaks highly of her husband and his secret missions abroad. Lainey is intrigued but her intuition tells her something is not right.

Even while her feelings for Max grow, Lainey can't help wondering about the charade being played at sea.

Additional Commentary:
The author doesn't like ending with a question, and I can respect that. I love how she works in the tie to her title each time. It adds a nice touch. The substitution of "woman" for "lady" works well too. The best blurb collaboration happens when the author takes the suggestions, processes them, and integrates it into a "voice" that fits the work.

More Blurbs I Helped Write:
Out of Her League by Shawn McGuire
Palm Trees and Snowflakes by Scott Bury

Bonus Case Study #1: First Person Blurb

First person blurbs are very rare. Usually, this is for good reasons. The book description needs to capture the entire essence of the story. Due to the nature of the first person perspective, it's harder to back up enough to get that overview. As with all things, they can be done, and they can be done well. However, I maintain that it should not be your first instinct.

To be fair, a first person blurb can demonstrate a strong character voice. There's merit to this if it's a likable voice. Given the wide variety of tastes out there, this would be a good way to weed out people who would not enjoy the main character's voice.

Title: *Enforcer*
Author: Kai Bertrand
Genre: Urban Fantasy

Author Synopsis:
It's a serial is about twin brothers, Cain and Ari, who were killed and brought back from the dead. They're given supernatural jobs to do. Ari becomes Death and Cain is an Enforcer. The first episode is written from the perspective of Cain. The second will be from Ari's POV, the third back to Cain. It's a snarky, supernatural journey for two brothers who thought they were human and find out they're not.

Original Blurb by Kai Bertrand:
It started with death, my own. It went downhill from there.

My name is Cain. I'm an Enforcer. I've been given the power to suggest you kill yourself. If the circumstances are right, you'll do it.

Our town is being taken over by demons. People are trapped in their own bodies with no way out. Possession. An Enforcer gives a possessed person one last chance to rid themselves of the demon controlling them. The separation process tends to be messy.

I hate being an enforcer. I could refuse to do it but it means I'll have to stand by and watch my friends and neighbors kill or be killed. My twin brother Ari tells me I'll get used to it. That's easy for him to say, he's Death. I'm a smartass with a deadly power. What were they thinking?

Follow Cain as he gets dragged kicking and screaming into the battle between Good and Evil.

Comments:
You need a stronger tagline. There's a nice rhythm to it, but it's choppy. Enforcer is capitalized some places and not in others. The last line abruptly switches tenses. I would advise against using first person in a blurb at all. I know it adds to the style, but it also leads to that sudden shift at the end.

The blurb raises the following questions:
What conditions need to be right for the Enforcer to work?
What does it mean "by chance?" What are the stipulations?
Do the Enforcers help with the separation?
Why would your reader care if Cain is a smartass?
Does Cain have a choice in being an Enforcer? What are the consequences if he doesn't become an Enforcer? (The reader doesn't know they died and were brought back. I know that because of your miniature synopsis.)

Suggested Rewrite:
(Town name) has been overrun by demons.

They possess people, trapping them inside their own bodies. Separation can be … messy.

That's where Cain comes in. As an Enforcer, he gives a possessed person one last chance at breaking away from an indwelling demon. Cain doesn't like his job, but he also can't stand by and watch friends and neighbors become monsters. His twin brother, Ari, also has a deadly gift.

Wise or not, higher powers have recruited Cain and Ari to be frontline fighters in the next great battle between Good and Evil.

Additional Commentary:
The author didn't like the suggested revision, but she said she would consider some of what I'd said moving forward as she did her rewrite.

Bonus Case Study #2: Successful Story

Let's examine something different, a blurb that's proven effective and see how it lines up with the things described in this book.

Proof of Success:

The book's been downloaded over a million times with over 200,000 sales before it went permanently free. It's spawned a 12-book series and attracted the attention of the Amazon Kindle Worlds people. The series has sold over a million copies. There's an entire Kindle World dedicated to the Lei Crime Series. That means that now, 50+ authors have written spin-off stories based on these characters. In short, it's successful. But anything good can be even better.

Title: *Blood Orchids*
Author: Toby Neal
Genre: Mystery

Original Blurb by Toby Neal: (I left it how I found it from Amazon)

From award-winning, bestselling author Toby Neal, whose writing Kirkus Reviews calls "persistently riveting," comes the Lei Crime Series!

Hawaii is palm trees, black sand and blue water—but for policewoman Lei Texeira, there's a dark side to paradise.

Lei has overcome a scarred past to make a life for herself as a cop in the sleepy Big Island town of Hilo. On a routine patrol she finds two murdered teenaged girls, one of whom she knows. The girl's harsh life and tragic death affect Lei deeply. She becomes obsessed with the case—even as the killer is drawn to Lei, feeding off her vulnerabilities and toying with her sanity.

Despite the circumstances, Lei finds herself falling for the lead detective, Michael Stevens.

The steaming volcanoes, black sand beaches and shrouded fern forests of Hawaii are the backdrop to Lei's quest for answers—and a killer is closer than she can imagine.

Fast-paced crime mystery with a touch of romance, readers call Blood Orchids "un-putdownable!"
"Sometimes in crime fiction you find a character who lives on beyond the book's end by virtue of their psychological complexity, and the richness with which the author has drawn them. Will Graham, Jack Reacher, and Alex Cross now have a worthy female counterpart in Lei Texeira. Blood Orchids satisfies on every level. A powerful new talent is on the scene, whole-heartedly recommended."
-Drew Cross, former police officer and author of BiteMarks

Analysis:
This blurb has a few things going for it that might not be available to the majority of indie authors.

1) It's got a statement at the top from a respected review company saying it's awesome.
2) It's got a quote that praises it courtesy of another author.
3) It's got some bold sections that draw your eye to the tagline and another quote that says "hey, this is great!"

The tagline seems on the long side, but the author has established a rhythm to the way she writes her taglines in this series. The lack of a space between the paragraphs makes the blurb harder to read. If the reader's not immediately dazzled by the strong praise, they may or may not finish the blurb. On the other hand, it is a nice length. "A scarred past" throws me off on first glance. Note how the author's nicely set the location and established the main character right away.

If there wasn't an established pattern to the tagline, I'd suggest something like: Her past comes with scars …

The last sentence doesn't fit the flow of the rest of the blurb. The part about Michael Stevens is interesting, but it's also not really jiving with the rest of the blurb. There's good symmetry between the last sentence and the tagline. (I keep calling it a tagline, but it's not really one. It's more accurate to say the opening statement.)

I love the phrase "dark side to paradise." It's beautiful and powerful.

I believe there are separate paragraphs here but the way it's spaced out turns it into a "big, ugly paragraph." The bold for the tagline definitely helps combat some of the effect by providing some contrast.

Suggested Rewrite:
Hawaii is palm trees, black sand, and blue water, but for policewoman Lei Texeira, there's a dark side to paradise.

Overcoming a past filled with scars, Lei makes a life for herself as a cop in the sleepy Big Island town of Hilo. When a routine patrol turns up two murdered teens, Lei's world is rocked. She knows one of the girls.

Even as Lei is drawn to the case, the killer's attention fixes on her.

Despite the strain of being toyed with by a murderer, Lei's attracted to the lead detective, Michael Stevens. But she can't afford distractions. Amidst an enchanting backdrop of Hawaii's black sand beaches and shrouded fern forests, a killer's closing in on her.

Commentary on the suggested rewrite:
The author will certainly want to leave the unique bells and whistles she's earned to date. My suggested changes are mainly about the flow. I've tried to make a mini-story out of the blurb that doesn't give too much away. This blurb already had so many things going for it, but I wanted to make the last two paragraphs seem more natural.

Aside on Endorsements and Review Quotes:
If your book's earned rewards or other accolades, you should definitely include them on the Amazon or other ebook retailer splash page, but I'd prefer they come after the blurb itself. That might just be a personal preference thing, but especially if it's an award I've never heard of, I don't really care about the story until I know what it's about.

If an author in that genre thinks your work is great, you should quote them if possible. The more marketing power they have, the better. "This book is awesome" does not have the same ring coming from you if you've written it. Authors do have to promote themselves, but it sounds more genuine coming from another person.

Chapter 7:
5 Steps to Better Blurbs

I call it "my method" but I highly doubt I invented it. This is simply a collection of the best advice I can give based on my experience with writing and rewriting blurbs for people. The general version that follows should be applicable to a wide range of genres and give you the ability to reach multiple generations of readers. If you search for "blurb writing" on Amazon, you'll come up with a half-dozen books on the topic. Find the one that works for you.

The tone of the blurb can differ from the book, but be careful about what impression you're leaving on the reader. I worked with a blurb once that was for a dark fantasy, but the way the original blurb came across, I got a distinct light-hearted urban fantasy vibe. If the tone you're setting isn't the one you want, you need to tweak your blurb.

And now, the moment you've all been waiting for ...

5 Steps to Better Blurbs:
Step #1: Tagline
Step #2: Introduction
Step #3: Elaboration/Complication
Step #4: Stakes
Step #5: Conclusion/Teaser

Step #1: Tagline
Regardless of genre, a tagline is vital to your blurb. It's the short statement or question that will snag the reader's attention. This may be the same or different than the tagline generated for the series or front cover of a paperback novel.

I'm surprised by the number of blurbs that lack a decent tagline. They can be tough to generate, but thinking of one is a great exercise for tuning your thoughts to writing the rest of the blurb.

They don't always have to be grammatically correct. Sometimes fragments work well. Imagine that you have five seconds to interest a person. What do you want them to know about your book? You should probably center the tagline on the main character, but this isn't a hard and fast rule.

If you're struggling to come up with one, do a little research on taglines for popular movies and books. You might gain some inspiration. Then, return to your work, give yourself a set time like ten minutes, and throw down as many phrases about your book as you can. When you review this list later, you may find the seeds of your tagline in there.

Step #2: Introduction

We need to meet the main character right away.

Who is the book about?

Try to balance the amount of information. As mentioned previously, your genre may dictate that the reader knows your protagonist's age. I'd done this instinctively with most of my early YA works, but it's always good to be purposeful about such things.

Don't overwhelm the reader. This is not the time to tell us hair and eye color unless it's a vital piece of the plot you're willing to share with the reader. You want to paint a brief picture of this person in your introduction.

What is the main character doing when the reader first meets them? Just as important as meeting the main character, the answer to this question will help the reader form a mental image of the wider world you've placed your main character in.

Try to keep this section to one small paragraph, maybe 3-5 sentences long.

Step #3: Elaboration/Complication
The elaboration/complication section is a great place to introduce a second main character or a villain. This is where you give the reader a few bits of insight as to what's wrong in the world you've been shaping.

What problems does the main character face? Is she being stalked? Is he being bullied? Is she struggling with an addiction? Is he afraid to tell a girl he likes her?

You want to introduce the conflict here, but don't go into too much detail. Remember, a blurb's an invitation to read on, not the summary of everything that the reader will encounter.

Step #4: Stakes
In mystery and thrillers, I often keep the stakes to a sentence or two immediately following the conflict. In essence, this is the culmination of the conflict. If the hero or heroine fails to accomplish their goal, what are the consequences? Is it a matter of life and death, a broken heart, or the end of the world?

The romance genre lends itself nicely to a stakes statement.

The stakes don't have to be earth-shattering. They simply have to be important to the protagonist. For example, losing a job or having to move won't change much of the rest of the world, but it has the potential to rock a character's life all the same. Saving a pet or watching a parent suffer from an incurable disease could also be stakes. The possibilities are endless.

Step #5: Conclusion/Teaser
Typically, this section boils down to a sentence or two. You need to finish up strong. You can end with a question, but do your best to not let it be something that can be given a simple "yes" or "no" answer.

Note: Sometimes Step 4 and Step 5 are combined together into one slightly longer paragraph. While it can be good to separate out the stakes part to make it stand on its own, it's not a set rule. If you're not sure if it's a good idea, try it both ways and see what some other people think of the spacing.

End with something meaningful. This is your last chance to impress a reader and excite them enough to grab your book.

Keep it Simple:
I've totally written longer blurbs, but they're not my best works. As I've improved the skill through practice, I've become more a fan of brevity.

Let's return to the goal for a moment. You want the reader to desire more of your book. People read a lot of stuff online. Respect their time and get your message across in a straightforward, manner. Not everybody who reads your blurb will buy the book, but that's okay. Likely, you don't want every reader to pick up your book if it's not "their thing."

How many times have you read a review where the reader complained about the content? You want to avoid this. I love clean mysteries and lighthearted, weird stuff, so if that's what you write, make sure your blurb tells me that's what I'm going to get. I avoid dark, depressing stuff, but if that's what you've written, tailor the blurb to blare that message. If the reader ends up with a book they don't like, nobody wins.

Chapter 8:
6 Exercises to Spiff Up Those Blurbs

I will try to get a Word doc and pdf version of this section prepped and posted to my website for those who wish to print hard copies or work with the files. (If I can't manage that, you can always request them the old-fashioned way, by email. Just let me know which version you need. Pdf or doc would work best.) These are 100% optional homework assignments. Skip to Exercise #6 if you want to dive into your own blurb, but remember, cutting corners can be dangerous and detrimental.

Exercise #1: Tangling with Taglines

Remember that taglines are different than summaries. These little beauties need to reach out, grab the reader, and hold him tight.

First Assignment: Write 3-5 different taglines for a movie/book you love. Note what emotion each evokes. Do this for a few different movies/books and compare them.

Example: Star Wars Episode VII: The Force Awakens
(Nostalgic) Old war. New heroes.
(Hopeful) Deepest dark shows the brightest light.
(Neutral/factual) Galactic fate favors a scavenger.

Second Assignment: Try writing 3-5 different taglines for your own book. As before, note the emotion contained in each attempt.

Exercise #2: Mini-Movie Snapshots

First Assignment: Sum up a movie/book you love in 20 words or less.

Second Assignment: Sum up that same movie/book you love in 15 words or less.

Example: Star Wars Episode IV: A New Hope – A farm boy saves a rebellion from annihilation through a mysterious Force. (12 words)

Exercise #3: Genre Genie

Assignment: Take the blurb for Awakening (middle grade, coming of age, fantasy) or one of your own and rewrite it so that it fits a brand new genre. Do this twice. Try making it something that's not a huge stretch like science fiction or horror first. Next, try making it something completely different like mystery or sweet romance. What would it look like as a Western?

Original Blurb for Awakening:
Being the Chosen One could kill her ...

Victoria Saveron knows two things for certain. Dark forces want to kill her, and her friends have cooler powers than she does. Katrina can shapeshift and Tellen can tap into destructive magic currents.

Everything else is uncertain and rumors abound.

Victoria might be the Chosen One, whatever that means. Her father might be able to help them, but only if they can find him. Coldhaven's villagers might be able to offer them food and shelter. Some fool might be running around unlocking Darkland portals to raise an undead army.

The further Victoria and her companions get on their journey, the more dangers and betrayals they face. They must awaken Vic's true powers or forfeit the world.

Example 1 *Awakening* **as Science Fiction:**
Being the Chosen One could kill her ...

On the far-off planet of Aeris, dark forces are rising, and only Victoria Saveron has the power to stem the tide of evil. Her two friends—Katrina and Tellen—must protect her long enough to awaken the power within her.

If they fail, the world is doomed.

Commentary:
Science fiction and fantasy are closely related genres, but they have very distinct differences. I don't think you could construe Awakening as a hard science fiction because it lacks all elements of the technology needed to become such, but I not interested in changing the story. I only want to fiddle with the words until it sounds like it could be a scifi book. The tagline from the original is still valid.

On the whole, science fiction and fantasy stories usually have a wider, more sweeping scope. The stakes tend to be all or nothing, save the world/doom the world. This should come through clearly in the blurb.

Certain words and phrases scream science fiction or fantasy. The following list is by no means comprehensive. I'm merely throwing some examples out there to prompt your minds. Likely, you already instinctively know most of these.

Words/phrases common to science fiction or fantasy:
Chosen One, hero, planet, darkness, evil, forces, king/queen, angel, demon, power, world, save, doom, ritual

Example 2 *Awakening* as a Mystery:
Death stalks her ...

While her father's away on business, Victoria Saveron and her two friends narrowly escape being killed in a surprise attack.

Who would want to kill a thirteen-year-old girl? Can Vic's two friends protect her from the evil that pursues her?

Words/phrases common to mystery: detective, victim, body, murder, missing, kidnapping, escape, protect, find, death

Commentary:
In a way, there are mystery elements in here, so this might not be too much of a stretch. To make it fit that genre a little better, I need to make word choices that downplay the supernatural and emphasize the mysterious aspects. Basically, you need to cut anything that would scream fantasy. Chosen One is definitely a hallmark of fantasy, so the tagline needs to be changed.

Note: The lists that follow are by no means comprehensive. They're merely meant to spark your imagination.

Try these genres:
Words/phrases common to historical fiction: lady, gentleman, brothel/ "lady of the night", dress, heir, king, land, lord, dispute, bandit, scoundrel, poor, common, slave

Words/phrases common to western: horse, ranch, cattle, range, prairie, gold, wagon, bandit, dust, snake, boots, sheriff, deputies, law, man, woman

Words/phrases common to horror: body, blood, ax, bat, zombie, apocalypse, murderer, insane, evil, creepy, haunted house, ghost, wolf, monster

Words/phrases common to romance: inheritance, scion, heir, dispute, class, love, lust, handsome/beautiful, desire, passion, presence, magnetic, billionaire

Words/phrases common to action/adventure: journey, discover, save, risk, fight, survive, lose, travel, lost, crash

Words/phrases common to dystopia: government, oppressive, totalitarian, evil, uniform, utopia, death, imprisonment, control, perfect, society, rise up, fight/battle, ordinary

Exercise #4: Generation Genie:

Assignment: Take the blurb for Awakening (YA, Coming of Age, Fantasy) or one of your own and rewrite it so that it's aimed at small children (like picture books). Next, fix it so that it appeals to adults.

Original Blurb for Awakening:
Being the Chosen One could kill her ...

Victoria Saveron knows two things for certain. Dark forces want to kill her, and her friends have cooler powers than she does. Katrina can shapeshift and Tellen can tap into destructive magic currents.

Everything else is uncertain and rumors abound.

Victoria might be the Chosen One, whatever that means. Her father might be able to help them, but only if they can find him. Coldhaven's villagers might be able to offer them food and shelter. Some fool might be running around unlocking Darkland portals to raise an undead army.

The further Victoria and her companions get on their journey, the more dangers and betrayals they face. They must awaken Vic's true powers or forfeit the world.

Commentary:
The original blurb has more of a flippant, casual tone than a lot of my other book descriptions. That lends itself nicely to the young adult genre because it demonstrates the tone of the book. "Cooler" is probably not a term I'd use if I want to appeal to adults.

Example 1 *Awakening* **for Children:**
Vic's in danger!

And only her friends can help her. Katrina's a shapeshifter and Tellen can control lightning, but will their special gifts be able to awaken Vic's powers too?

Will the journey to Coldhaven draw the friends together, or will betrayal ruin everything?

Commentary:
The violence has been downplayed. The exclamation point makes it urgent but also a tad more light-hearted. Mentioning that Katrina's a shapeshifter and Tellen too has a gift is appropriate because children's books are more open to odd things coming and going. Imagination and fantasy enter and exit these stories at will.

"Ruin everything" is extremely vague. Coldhaven hints at it being fantasy. The phrase "draw the friends together" makes it sound more like this is mainly about the dynamics of their friendship. That theme is more appropriate to the children's book genre.

Example 2 *Awakening* for Adults:
Being the Chosen One could kill her ...

Dark forces want Victoria Saveron dead. And neither she, nor her two friends, can fathom why. They have useful powers like shapeshifting and controlling lightning, while she merely lights up when danger draws near.

They need to find her father. He should have answers.

The further Vic and her companions get on their journey, the more dangers and betrayals they face. Little do they know that Vic's untapped powers are all that stand between the world and an army of undead about to rise.

Commentary:
Not too much has changed. I lost the section with all the "mights." I removed the phrase "some fool." I took something akin to a mystery approach in framing this blurb. I shortened the sentences and tweaked it so that more things came out in a direct tone.

Exercise #5: Stakes Identifier

Assignment: Take a favorite movie or book and identify the stakes faced by the main character(s). You can lay it out as an if/then statement.

Example: Star Wars Episode VII: The Force Awakens – If Rey and Finn don't get BB-8 to the Resistance, then Luke Skywalker may never be found.

Second Example: Star Wars Rogue One – If Jyn, Cassian, and the Rebel Alliance can't recover the Death Star plans, the Empire will unleash it's planet killer on the galaxy.

Note: You probably don't always want to state the stakes in your blurb as an if/then statement, but it will help you identify where to start with that section.

Exercise #6: Lay it All Out in 1 Page

Let's get down to business and focus on your blurb. Here are some questions to answer. Check my website for a blank version. Please notice the amount of space you have for each question. Try to stick within this space. We can beat this into a coherent blurb later.

Blurb Focusing Tool:
1. What is your genre? Who is your target audience? My ideal customer is ...
2. What is your tagline?
3. Who is/are your main characters?
4. What makes your book awesome? (selling points)
5. Are there any secrets revealed in the book you want to keep from the readers for now?
6. Who are the other important characters? What makes them special? Do you want them in the blurb? Imagine you had to pay $5 for each character you included in the description.
7. What's the tone of the story? Do you want the same tone in your blurb?
8. What are the stakes?
9. Main Points – Say what you need to say in 5 bullet points or less.
   - MP 1 –
   - MP 2 –
   - MP 3 –
   - MP 4 –
   - MP 5 –

Draft Your Blurb:
Take the things you wrote when you laid it all out and stuff it into paragraph form. This is the ugly draft. We're going to scrap it and start over soon, but it should at least have given you an idea of where you want to take this miniature advertisement for your book.

Refine Your Draft Two Ways:
I suggest doing this part in a word processor. Copy/paste your ugly blurb twice. Select your favorite tagline for your current work and let that set the tone for what comes in your first refinement. Select a different tagline with a separate emotional push and see where that one leads.

Analyze the two drafts with the following questions and focal points:
Write down any phrases from either version that you absolutely love and definitely want to keep.
Which version captures your attention better?
Which draft leaves you wanting more?

Write a new draft with the best from both previous drafts. Ask yourself ...
Does it flow?
Did I adequately introduce the key players to the reader?
Does it give enough information without giving too much away?

Chapter 9:
Adapting the Blurb for Different Situations

"[This chapter] is a good set of mental exercises that can also help people to be less attached to their sacred written words, a problem every writer has."
~C. M. Barrett, Author of *The Dragon Who Didn't Fly*

Consider Case Study #6 *Joss the Seven*. You'll recall that the author provided me with five different versions of his blurb. As if writing the blurb once wasn't traumatic enough for some people, it's often necessary to adapt the book description to fit different advertising and spacing needs. For example, *Heartfelt Cases* started out as a series of novellas. They're still sold separately today, but I also have a combination book in paperback which required new blurbs. Slapping the ebook versions of the book descriptions onto the back cover required going to a ridiculously small font to fit everything. That's not always the best solution.

Paperback vs. Ebook:

I have a tendency to call a blurb the back cover copy even though more often than not I'm referring to the description posted to the product page. The original blurb (second draft) I had for *Ashlynn's Dreams* fits very nicely on the back cover of the 6x9 paperback version, so I probably won't change it for that. I checked the *Heartfelt Cases Books 1-3* collection and discovered that I'd left the original blurbs there. They barely fit. Uploading the new version to that will help, but I could also adjust everything. I may do so anyway just for the sake of demonstrating.

The paperback blurb is 195 words. The rewrite for ebook retailers is 80 words. Personally, I think having only 80 words would leave too much space on the back cover. A few years ago, the idea of having different blurbs for the paperback and the ebook would have caused my insides to coil. Now, I think it's necessary or at least acceptable and understandable.

Blurbs for a Collection:

The back cover of *Heartfelt Cases Books 1-3* is currently the collection of the individual blurbs. It clocks in at 298 words, which is massive. On the paperback, it looks all right, but adjustments can be made to make it shorter and snappier. While I believe one can "get away with" long descriptions on a paperback, it's a worthwhile exercise to make the adjustments and see what the blurbs could be.

Original Description for *Heartfelt Cases Books 1-3*:
Book 1: The Collins Case:
A young family disappears …

FBI Special Agent Julie Ann Davidson isn't assigned the case, but she works it anyway because she knows the Collins family. Add in a baffling case of internet thievery, and Ann and her partner, Patrick Duncan, have plenty to think about.

Who took the Collins family and why?

One thing's certain: time is running out.

If Ann and Patrick don't work fast, Rachel Collins and her kids will die.

Book 2: The Kiverson Case:
One man's vendetta could cost them everything …

When a routine arrest turns deadly, FBI Special Agents Julie Ann and Patrick Duncan are drawn into a dangerous game with Kevin Kiverson, a man with little to lose and much to avenge.

In her heart, Ann knows they will catch Kevin, but she doesn't know when or how or what sacrifices will be made along the way. She's prepared to risk her life for others but will her resolve hold when the threat turns to her baby boy? Book 3: The Davidson Case:
Somebody wants her sister dead ...

FBI Special Agent Ann Duncan knows how to face down danger, but once again, she's not the target. Her baby sister, Joy Davidson, has stumbled upon a conspiracy and made some powerful enemies.

Luck and God's grace help Ann save her sister the first time, but she knows the bad guys will try again. With Patrick on a university tour and perhaps the most important case of her career weighing upon her mind, Ann must find the strength, wisdom, and heart to find out who wants her sister dead, what Joy discovered, and how to stop the conspirators.

Ann instinctively knows that if she fails the Davidson case will only be the first of many tragedies.

Comments:
There are a couple of ways to approach a collection like this. I can write a blurb for the whole thing or I can gear it toward the individual stories. This holds true for any short story collection. I've chosen to gear this toward the individual stories, but I've seen it done well as an overview of the collection.

Possible Rewrite 1 (individual stories): 162 words
Book 1: The Collins Case:

A young family disappears …

FBI Special Agents Julie Ann Davidson and Patrick Duncan race against time to find a missing mother and two children.

One thing's certain: if they don't work fast, the Collins family is doomed.

Book 2: The Kiverson Case:
One man's vendetta could cost them everything …
When a routine arrest turns deadly, FBI Special Agents Julie Ann and Patrick Duncan are drawn into a dangerous game with Kevin Kiverson, a man with little to lose and much to avenge.

Ann's prepared to risk her life but will her resolve hold when the threat turns to her baby boy?

Book 3: The Davidson Case:
Somebody wants her sister dead …

FBI Special Agent Ann Duncan knows how to face down danger, but once again, she's not the target. Her baby sister, Joy, has made some powerful enemies.

Ann knows that if she fails, her sister might only be the first victim of many.

Possible Rewrite 2 (whole collection): 77 words
2 agents, 3 cases, 1 God …
Ann and Patrick aren't your typical FBI agents, but then again, these aren't normal cases either.

They're much more personal.

The Collins Case: The agents race against time to find one of Ann's high school friends.

The Kiverson Case: Ann and Patrick battle a man bent on revenge.
The Davidson Case: Ann scrambles to find out who wants her sister dead.

Fear rules their world, will it rule their hearts?

Comments:

I would choose rewrite 1 for a new paperback version and rewrite 2 for an ebook retailers. Way back when *Heartfelt Cases* was published by one of those old-school, self-publishing companies, I'd used the last line as a tagline on the front of the book. Ending with a tagline isn't normal, but it's doable here because the style of rewrite 2 is oriented to the "big picture." I might seek to change the back cover copy of the paperback. It's just a tad harder because I need to ask the original cover artist to tweak the pdf file.

Giving Your Book Social Media Legs:

If you want to be super thorough, you should probably have a 10-15 word version, 25-word version, 50-word version, and a 75-word version in addition to your normal blurb. The soon-to-be current version of The Collins Case comes to 79 words, and the abbreviated one amounts to 49 words.

Twitter's all about brevity. According to AdEsspresso, Facebook ads have three sections for ad copy: headline, text, and newsfeed link description. Coming up with a great headline is probably most similar to generating a tagline, but in this section, I'm going to focus on the main text. I'm not sure exactly how many words you're allowed. Like twitter, it's probably more about the number of characters than actual word count, but you can assume that short and catchy ad copy will fare better than ad copy that is not.

As you tighten the wording, you need to keep distilling down the essence of the story until you have only the facts. There's no time for flowery prose. Flowery tends to equate to wordy.

Let's try a 25-word version and a 10-word version.

The Collins Case in <25 words:

A young family disappears, and one thing's certain: if the FBI agents don't work fast, the Collins family is doomed.

Note: If you plug the above into twitter, you have a grand total of 24 characters left to play with. It's still too long. It might suffice for a Facebook ad though.

The Collins Case in <10 words:
2 FBI agents race to rescue a kidnapped family.

Note: This one is Twitter-friendly.

How do you go about making such changes?
While there's no ready "this will always work" answer, bear in mind that you're trying to get to the heart and soul of your story. Spend less time worrying about name dropping and more time thinking of the big picture.

Try this approach:
Copy-paste your original blurb to a new document. Or write it down with a pen if you really want to get daring. I suggest the computer version because it's easier to manipulate words that way, but I also realize some people are satisfied by physically crossing things out as they go.

Read over what you have without stopping, then go back and read it again slowly. Pause over every part you think is an unnecessary detail. Names, places, anecdotal descriptions, and similar things should go. Either cross them out or delete them.

Rewrite what you have without the things you decided weren't absolutely necessary to your description.

You may have to add a few words to make the transitions smooth again.

Repeat the process until you're satisfied with the word count.

Some questions to think about that might help you focus:

What is the story about in a word or a phrase? (For example, a kidnapping, a murder, a lost love, a new love, a kingdom in peril, an epic journey home, finding lost __, a quest to survive)

Who is the story about? (a kidnapped child, an overworked detective, star-crossed lovers, a disgraced knight, a pair of lost kittens, sailors caught out in a storm)

What phrases from your original blurb do you really want to keep?

Chapter 10:
The Case for Stepping Back and Letting Go

Benefits to an Outsider's Perspective:

You love your story. You wouldn't be trying to publish the manuscript and get strangers to read it if you didn't believe in the plot and characters. When it comes to your blurb, you might need an outsider's perspective. You know exactly what you're talking about. The true test will be if somebody else understands what you're getting at and catches the vision for your story.

Free Options:

Most critique groups or forums will have a section where you can solicit advice. The smaller and more active a group is, the better quality of help you'll probably find there. Bigger groups are great too, but when you get thousands of people, you also run the risk of disappearing into the crowd.

Have some friendly strangers test drive your book blurb. Ask them what's working for them and what's not working? Where are they confused? In a pinch, family members work too, but you also need the unbiased opinion of somebody out of smacking range.

Still need help?

Many people, like me, will hire out their services as a blurbologist. Yes, that's really a thing. (I Googled it, so it must be true.)

Please refer to my website for current rates as these are subject to change.

Book Blurb Rewrite:
You already have a rough draft of your blurb. I will comment on the original blurb, offer a suggested rewrite, and tweak that rewrite once based on your comments. See the Case Studies section to see examples of how this pans out.

Book Description Generation from Notes:
This takes a lot more work, hence it's more expensive. I work with the raw notes to write a description for you then rewrite it based on your feedback.

As of this second, the rates are as follows:
$20 Blurb Rewrite + 1 revision
$40 Blurb Generation + 1 revision
$10 Revision Package - Up to 3 more revisions can be added to either package.
*You get $5 by buying this book. You could link to a review or send a screenshot of the page thanking you for the purchase. Any other proof of purchase, including, "Hey, I bought the book on __ date" would also work.

Fine Print: discount codes and offers do not stack. Sorry, but if that were the case, I'd probably owe you money.

How it Works:
You email me at devyaschildren@gmail.com, and let me know what you'd like (a rewrite or blurb generation). Also, let me know if you want a paypal invoice, a paypal.me link, or if you just want to send the money through to the email as a friend.

I'll get back to you with a rough time estimate and the invoice if you've asked for one. Once the details are worked out, you send your draft, title, genre, and any story notes you think will help me shape your blurb. After I've tackled your project, I'll send you a Word doc with the original, my comments, and my suggested rewrite. Once you comment on the suggested rewrite, I will make some adjustments and send it back to you. Final adjustments are always up to you.

I've also reworked people's About Me blurbs for online profiles and even done a non-fiction project or two, but my specialties are mystery and most genre fiction. I do not do erotica or creepy horror.

I'm always on the lookout for new case studies, so there will be frequent giveaways for people to win free blurb overhauls. Join my Book Blurb Club for the latest news on such giveaways. You can find the link to that on my website http://www.juliecgilbert.com/ or find the FB group first. The link should be there. FB search term: Julie C. Gilbert's Book Blurb Club.

Do I guarantee 100% satisfaction?
Tricky question.

Short answer: No.

Slightly longer answer: No, there are too many variables to control.

Much longer answer: I would love to believe that everybody would embrace and cherish the changes I suggest. In reality, most do like what I come up with and accept the bulk of the suggestions. But the nature of the blurb writing beast is such that one person's opinion my not truly resonate with another. Your goal in writing a stronger blurb is to attract and please the largest percentage of the people who lay eyes on your description.

This is an art, not a science. On the subject of traditional visual arts like paintings, I'll be the first to admit that there are a lot of really famous pieces worth millions of dollars that I think are downright ugly. Conversely, there are $10 sketches thrown together by friends I could stare at for a long time because they hold sentimental value for me. As for science, even in that evidence-based realm there are multiple ways to interpret data.

If you're not happy with the suggestions ...
You might need to face the reality that you're still too close to the work. I totally understand that. Until recently, my blurbs haven't changed for years. We become attached to certain ways of phrasing things, so when somebody says it could be better, there's a certain level of pain involved.

You have choices ...
You can find a forum or Facebook group and test the various blurbs. Writing groups are notoriously opinionated. If you post any blurb up on a Facebook group, it'd be a miracle if you don't have people offering suggestions. Take these opinions with a grain of caution. Many times, you'll get completely opposite advice. (You should see the discussion thread for the cover of this book.) If you want a hair more clarity, post it as a poll in several different places and just look at the results.

You can work with the suggested rewrite anyway, modifying things so that you're happy with the wording.

You could also simply scrap the suggestion and start from scratch with your synopsis and the principles described in this book.

You know your story best, but bear in mind that you're not writing the book description for yourself. You need it to attract others.

Encouragement:

You can do this! One can improve the art of blurb writing by practicing. Some of the stepping back you might have to do can be accomplished by taking a few hours or days off and then reading what you've written with fresh eyes. I still recommend seeing what some friendly strangers think of your blurb. Gather a bunch of opinions and then take the best of the advice and discard the rest.

How do you choose the "best" advice?

Some things will simply resonate with you. At other times, it's really difficult to parse good from bad advice. When in doubt, ask more questions. If you want to go about it the scientific way, write two different versions and A/B test them on some patient people. It takes longer, but you could also test them over time. It's hard to run an experiment when so many things could be influencing the outcomes, but you should get a decent idea of what works for your audience. You could even go as far as running ads with the different word choices.

Try keeping a log:

If you want to chronicle the journey, keep every major permutation of the blurb as it forms and number them. This way, you can watch the baby blurb as it's formed. Later, if something's not feeling right, you can also return to an earlier draft and begin your tinkering process anew.

Conclusion:

Book blurbs don't have to be scary. They take some practice, but one of the best parts about writing is that it's a skill that grows with time and in conjunction with the amount you do it. I will reiterate that an outsider can usually give you great insight into where and when a blurb isn't connecting, but think of the process as a fun challenge rather than something to avoid at all costs.

Thanks for reading! Hope you've learned how to make your blurbs better.

Sincerely,

Julie C. Gilbert

P.S. Reviews make the indie world go round. If you've found this information useful, please consider leaving a review.

Endorsements:

"Julie has the eye and ear to take an author's idea from ordinary blurb to one that captures the essence of a story and the reader's imagination."
~ Janet Oakley, LCKW – *Saddle Road* and *Coconut Island*

"Julie is the Blurb Queen, able to polish and refine the author's content into prose that POPS."
~ Amy Shojai, Lei Crime Kindle World - *Born to Love*

"Julie has the ability to distill an author's idea into a statement that makes readers want to open the book."
~ Scott Bury, LCKW - *Torn Roots*

"Julie is AWESOME at taking a nothing blurb and turning it into something completely excellent!!!"

~Amy Allen Hallmark, LCKW – *New Beginnings*

THE END
Go forth and write awesomeness.

Notes:

44618589R00058

Made in the USA
Middletown, DE
12 June 2017